THEN AND THERE SERIES
GENERAL EDITOR
MARJORIE REEVES

The Highland Clearances

FINLAY McKICHAN

Illustrated from contemporary

LONGMAN

LONGMAN GROUP UK LIMITED
Longman House,
Burnt Mill, Harlow, Essex CM20 2JE, England
and Associated Companies throughout the world.

First published 1977
Sixth impression 1987
ISBN 0 582 20541 7

Produced by Longman Group (FE) Ltd
Printed in Hong Kong

ISBN 0 582 20541 7

For Joan

Contents

To the Reader

All over the world there are people whose families in the first place came from the Highlands of Scotland. In the Scottish Lowlands, England, Canada, the United States of America, Australia, New Zealand and many other places you can look up the telephone directory and find people whose names begin with 'Mac'. Many of these are Highland names. For over two hundred years Highlanders have been leaving home to make a new life in the bustling factories of a great town, or to farm the wide plains of some land across the seas. It was between the 1770s and the 1870s that most had to make this move. They often left behind them a valley or a lochside, now deserted except for a shepherd or gamekeeper, which had once been home for many families. They were sad, and often bitter, that they had to go. They passed down to their children and grandchildren stories about what had happened. These stories show how angry they were about 'the Highland Clearances', as they came to be known. Their stories often blame the landowners, and tell of families being cruelly thrown off the land so that a greedy owner could get a higher rent by bringing sheep or deer onto his land in place of people.

In this book we try to find out what really happened. There is no doubt that the Highlanders left home. But why did they go? How many were forced to leave by the landowners? Were all the landowners cruel? And what did it feel like for Highlanders to move from land their families had farmed for as long as they could remember and go instead to what some of them called 'the land of strangers'? To answer these questions we have to start by finding out what it was like to live in the Highlands about 200 or 250 years ago.

Words printed in *italics* are explained in the Glossary, p. 94.

1 *The Changing Highlands*

Captain Edward Burt came to the Highlands of Scotland about 1730. He was an engineer officer in the Army and helped to make roads and bridges. These were to make it possible for the British Army to put down the Highlanders if they rebelled again against King George, as they had done in 1715. Captain Burt wrote long letters to a friend in London, describing what life was like in a country which few strangers then cared to visit. It was very different from England, and even from the Lowlands of Scotland. It had different ways of life, and the common language was Gaelic, not English. A traveller might easily take a week to reach Inverness from Glasgow and two or three weeks to get there from London. In bad weather it might take longer.

It was a dangerous country. One English officer met a Highland chief and drank whisky with him. They began to argue and became angry. One of the chief's followers, who only spoke Gaelic and did not understand English, thought that the officer must be insulting his chief, drew his pistol and fired it at the officer's head. Luckily for the officer, the pistol misfired. To insult a chief before one of his *clansmen* would cause a quarrel which might end in wounds or death. Highlanders were taught that their most important duty was to love their chief. One chief whom Captain Burt knew well was wounded in battle. After he had fallen, the enemy kept firing at him. He told his servant to escape, but the servant asked what they would think of him at home if he fled. He then lay down on top of the chief and, in shielding him, the servant himself got several wounds.

Captain Burt explained to his London friend that the 5

A Highland chief

Highlander would do so much for his chief because he thought of the *clan* as a huge family. He believed the clansmen were the children of the man who had founded the clan in distant times. He had been the first chief. His son had become the second chief, and so on till the present chief. He should therefore be given great respect and unquestioning obedience. He would decide when the clan should go to war, and would call out his men by sending round the 'fiery cross', two sticks tied together and burnt at the ends, together with written orders telling them where to meet. This summons would bring out men who had been trained from boyhood to be fierce and hardy warriors. Captain Burt was so impressed by the hardiness of the clansmen that he assured his friend that:

> When the Highlanders have to lie among the hills in cold, dry, windy weather, they sometimes soak the plaid [the tartan blanket which was their main garment] in some river or burn, and then holding up a corner of it a little above their heads, they turn themselves round and round in it. Then they lay themselves down on the heather, where the wet and warmth of their bodies make a steam like that of a boiling kettle. The wet they say keeps them warm by thickening the stuff and keeping the wind out.

By Captain Burt's time the chief no longer sent round the fiery cross to call his men to fight a battle with a rival clan. But the clansmen were still brought up to be warriors, and when Charles Edward Stuart ('Bonnie Prince Charlie') arrived from France in 1745 to start a rebellion, he was able to gather an army very quickly when orders were sent out by the chiefs who supported him (many did not). Many of the clansmen had been kept in training by cattle raids. Captain Burt knew a lot about these. He wrote that:

> The stealing of cows they call lifting, a softening word for theft. They go out in parties from ten to thirty men and cross large *tracts* of mountains till they arrive at the place, as far as they can from their homes, which they intend to raid. The principal time for this wicked practice is the *Michaelmas* Moon, when the cattle are in condition fit for markets. They drive the stolen cows in the night time, and by day they lie concealed among the mountains or in woods.

The chief divided among his clansmen those parts of the clan lands which could be farmed. They lived mainly on oats, 7

and these could usually be grown only along the foot of the valleys which divided the high mountains and on the flat land at the head of the sea *lochs*. In these places the Highlanders built the farm townships in which they lived. It was usually impossible to grow enough oats to feed the families for a full year. Oats had to be bought in from the Lowlands, and to pay for these (and sometimes for the rent) it was vital for the *tenants* to get a good price for the black cattle which they grazed on the pastures round the township. These were fattened on the sweet summer grass and in the early autumn driven down to the cattle fairs on the borders of the Lowlands, like that at Crieff. Captain Burt described what it was like to see the cattle being driven south:

> It was in a time of rain, by a wide river, where there was a boat to ferry over the drovers. The cows were about fifty in number, and took the water like spaniels, and when they were in, their Drivers made a hideous cry to urge them forwards; this, they told me, they did to keep those at the front from turning round, for in that case the rest would do the same, and then they would be in danger of being driven away and drowned by the torrent. I thought it a very odd sight to see so many noses and eyes just above water, and nothing of them more to be seen, for they had no horns.

During the rain, wind and snow of winter the Highlanders were almost trapped in their *townships*. Then, as Burt put it,

> They sit brooding in the smoke over the fire till their legs and thighs are scorched, and many have sore eyes, and some are quite blind. The smoke makes them almost as black as chimney-sweepers, and when the huts are not water-tight, which is often the case, the rain comes through the roof and, mixing with the sootiness of the inside, falls in drops like ink.

Opposite: *A farm township in the Highlands about 250 years ago*

A family at Ruthven, Invernesshire, by the fireside of their black house. The men on the left hand side are French travellers

Opposite: *Drovers loading cattle at Kyleakin, Skye*

There was little to look forward to in the coming of spring, for by then last summer's oats were running very short. Burt knew that 'this is a bad season with them, for then they bleed their cattle and boil the blood into cakes, which, together with a little milk and a short allowance of oatmeal, is their food'.

In a hungry spring, when food ran out, the chief often helped his men. It was his duty to protect the clan in war and peace. He would sometimes give out oats or even allow old or ill clansmen to stay in his household for the rest of their lives. If necessary, he might excuse some tenants from paying rent for their land. At least part of the rent was paid, not in money, but in *kind*, that is in foodstuffs such as oats, chickens, fish and sheep. If the chief was prepared to do without the rent from time to time, it was not only from kindness for his clansmen. It was also because he wanted to keep as many fighting men as possible around him. One chief, when asked what rent his land raised, replied that it raised 500 men.

THE DECLINE OF THE CLAN

As early as 1730 Captain Burt saw that the chief and his clansmen were not as close together and friendly as they had once been. One chief was ashamed, in front of an important Englishman, to shake his ragged clansmen by the hand, as they expected. A group of clansmen complained when their chief asked them to work for him for sixpence a day at a time when they could earn sixteen pence building the military roads. The chief told Captain Burt that if they had done this in the past they would have been thrown off the nearest rock. But by 1730 some Highlanders were beginning to copy the ways of the wealthier but more selfish Lowlanders. Many more did so after Prince Charles Edward and the clans which fought for him were finally defeated at the Battle of Culloden in 1746.

King George's government was determined to make sure that the Highlanders would never again have the chance to rebel. The clan must be destroyed as a fighting unit. Many clan warriors were in fact killed at Culloden and in the hunt which followed the battle. To make sure that new ones would not be given weapons or trained to fight, Parliament passed Disarming Acts. Highlanders were not allowed to carry firearms or wear Highland dress or play the pipes. One clansman was actually executed at Carlisle for 'playing the bagpipes, a weapon of war'. The aim was to make them forget, not only fighting, but also the clan itself, of which the colour of their plaid and the tunes played on the pipes would always remind them. The chiefs who had not lost their lands or been executed were no longer allowed to hold their own courts to try their clansmen. The Government wanted the Highlanders to forget their clans and their chiefs. They did not do this, but a chief

Opposite: *Eighteenth-century engraving of the Battle of Culloden, 1746*

did have to accept that he no longer had a private army which would turn out to fight when he sent round the fiery cross and that it was now more difficult to get his clansmen to do exactly what he wanted. It was a sad blow to him. He could no longer act as the monarch of his own little kingdom in the Highlands. But he might be able instead to enjoy, like the Lowland and English landowner, the fashionable society of Edinburgh or London, living in a fine house, wearing expensive clothes and eating rich food. To do this he would need more money. He might be able to get it from his tenants. If they could no longer fight for him, they might be able instead to pay much higher rents and pay them regularly. The chiefs did not all take up this idea soon after Culloden, but gradually many of them began to see their clansmen as payers of rent, rather than as fighters.

POPULATION INCREASE

Within a few years of the Battle of Culloden the number of people living in the Highlands began to rise rapidly and continued to do so for almost a hundred years. You can see this by looking at these figures for the four main Highland counties:

County	Population		
	1755	1801	1841
Argyll	66,286	81,277	97,371
Inverness	59,563	72,672	97,799
Ross and Cromarty	48,084	56,318	78,685
Sutherland	20,744	23,117	24,782

We do not know exactly what were the reasons for this. Probably the most important was that doctors were using new methods which meant that fewer children died. What we can work out is what this meant for the ordinary Highlander. Look at the plan opposite which shows three farm townships on the island of Tiree as they were in 1769. You can see the cluster of houses on each farm in which the tenants and their families lived. They did not have their own separate plots, but shared the land and co-operated in working it. The table on page

14

16 shows that there were also men called cottars. They did not pay rent direct to the landlord. They would work for the tenants by helping to plough the fields, harvest the crops, herd the cattle and cut *peat* to burn during the winter. In return, they would be given a little piece of land on which to grow oats or potatoes. They might also pay a small rent to one of the tenants.

In these *townships* between the 1760s and the 1780s many tenants and cottars had large families. More of the boys than ever before lived to become men and soon they wanted to marry and start families of their own. Their fathers hated the idea of forcing them to leave the place where they had been brought up, and so they allowed them part of the land around the township. You can see from the table how many extra people there were in the township by 1792, when a count was made

A map showing the townships of Scarinish, Hianish and Baugh, Tiree, 1769

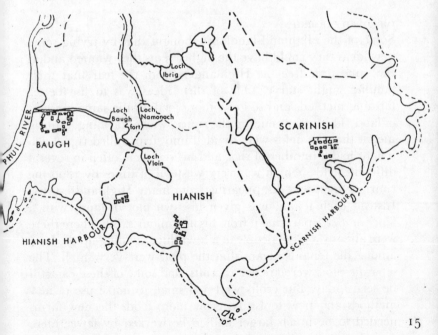

for the landowner, the Duke of Argyll. But there was no extra land. Most men were having to provide for their families from a smaller amount of land than their fathers or grandfathers had. What would happen if more and more people had to live on this land? Would the year come when, after a bad harvest, some of them would starve? And how could the landlords get the higher rents they wanted to pay for fine houses and rich clothes when so many more poor families were being fed from the same amount of land?

Farm	1769			1792
	Tenants	Cottars	Total population	Total population
Baugh	6	9	62	104
Hianish	4	6	36	53
Scarinish	10	8	58	96

IMPROVED FARMING

Some of the Highland landlords thought that by trying some new ideas they could have the higher rents they wanted and at the same time free the Highlanders from the fear that their families might starve. One of their ideas was to use better farming methods and so grow more food on the same amount of land. This meant ending the runrig way of farming. Runrig meant that the fields were divided into strips called rigs. Each tenant had a number of rigs, and his rigs were often in several different fields, which was very wasteful of time. By 1800 the runrig system was disappearing from many Highland estates. Instead each tenant was given his own plot of land, with a fence or *dyke* separating it from his neighbour's. But where there were already a lot of people in a township, dividing up the land among the tenants meant that the plots were very small. The separate plots were known as crofts, and some of these can still be seen today. But crofts were too small to make use of new methods and new tools. To grow more food, the new farms needed to be much larger and to be worked by fewer men.

What could be done with the tenants who would be pushed out if larger farms were set up?

FISHING

One idea was that the Highlanders ought to learn to catch fish. A landowner wrote that 'the seas abound with fish, the Highlands with hard working and good people. It will be our business to bring these two to meet.' He and other landowners set up the British Fisheries Society in 1786. As most of them spent the greater part of the year in London, that was where their meetings were held. They would come together at Waghorn's Coffee House, sometimes as often as once a week, and decide how fishing villages were to be set up in far away places: at Tobermory (Mull), Loch Bay (Skye) and Ullapool (Wester

The British Fisheries Society's stations were not the only ones. This one was at Tanera Mor in the Summer Isles, Ross-shire

Ross) on the west coast, and at Wick (Caithness) in the east. They worked very hard and even worried over little things, such as how the chimneys of the inn at Ullapool could be prevented from smoking. But, except at Wick, they were unable to make the Highlanders into successful fishermen. The people in the other villages were more interested in growing oats and potatoes on the little crofts the Society gave them. This was not only because they were unwilling to try something new. In the 1790s, when the Society's villages on the west coast were being built, the herrings it hoped the Highlanders would catch were very hard to find. And in trying to find them, fishermen were sometimes captured by French *privateers* or by the *press gang* of a British man of war. It was safer to dig the croft.

TEXTILES

A few highland landowners and lowland business men tried to encourage the making of linen, woollen and cotton goods in the Highlands. The bravest attempt was at Spinningdale, on the Dornoch Firth. There in 1792 a large cotton mill was built in the style of a medieval castle by George Dempster, the landowner, and by David Dale, Glasgow's leading cotton spinner. But it was too far to the towns in the south where most of the cotton had to be sold, and when the mill was burned about 1809 it was not rebuilt. The same problem defeated other men who were trying then to help the Highlander to earn a living by spinning and weaving.

KELP

Although many of them tried, it was not easy for landowners to make money and at the same time give the Highlanders work. You may be surprised to know that one way in which this could be done was by burning seaweed! (*Kelp*). Seaweed ash was a form of soda. It was in great demand to make glass and soap because the war with France cut off supplies of foreign soda. It cost between £3 and £4 a ton to make and send south and for a few years after 1800 was sold at from £10 to £20 per ton. Most of the profit went to the landowner, but a large number of Highlanders could earn something by helping to collect and burn the kelp. This was hard work and many hands were needed to get it done. James Robertson, who travelled through Inverness-shire at this time, explained why:

> The kelp-cutters tied it with ropes, in large bunches, waiting the approach of the tide, by which it is usually floated ashore, or sometimes carried on horses from among the rocks. Then it is spread to dry for two or three days and afterwards put into the *kiln*. It is set on fire and fed till the kiln be full of ashes. The kelp is then stirred into a liquid mass, without stopping, until it becomes stiff, which is very hard labour. Then a second and a third and sometimes a fourth layer is put on top.

There was one other way in which the landowner could make more money: by bringing in the great sheep.

2 The Great Sheep

The Highlanders had kept sheep for a long time. Their sheep had straight horns and coats of different colours, black, white, grey or brown. Highland sheep were treated almost like pets. They were taken indoors at night for shelter and were given names by their owners. But they were often badly fed and so were usually small and thin. The best grass was kept for the cattle, which had to be sold to buy oats and pay the rent. The sheep were not used to earn money, but simply to meet the needs of the owner and his family. They would drink the sheep's milk, wear clothes made of their wool and, occasionally, when one was killed, eat a dish of mutton.

THE BLACKFACED SHEEP

After 1760 a very different kind of sheep began to graze on Highland hills. It was the Linton or blackfaced sheep. Its face and legs were black and its coat white. It had been carefully bred in the Tweeddale country in the Scottish borders to make as much money as possible for its owners. It was hardy enough to find its own food for most of the year in the hills and its excellent mutton sold for high prices. The border sheep farmers looked round for wide pastures which could carry large flocks of Lintons. In the years after 1760 they found such pastures in the hilly country between the northern shores of the Firth of Clyde and the foot of Loch Ness. They would ride across the hills, then call on the local landowner to offer him a high rent if he would allow them to bring in their blackfaced sheep. The

Opposite: *This map shows the advance of the great sheep through Scotland*

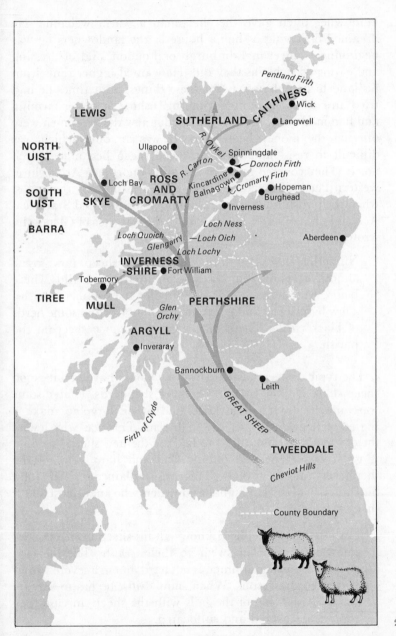

Pentland Firth

CAITHNESS
SUTHERLAND
● Wick
● Langwell

LEWIS

NORTH
UIST

Ullapool ●   Spinningdale
R. Oykel
R. Carron   → Dornoch Firth
ROSS   Kincardine
AND   Balnagown
CROMARTY   ← Cromarty Firth
● Loch Bay   ● Hopeman
SKYE   Burghead
● Inverness

SOUTH
UIST

BARRA

Loch Ness
Loch Quoich   — Loch Oich
Glengarry   Loch Lochy

INVERNESS
-SHIRE ● Fort William

● Aberdeen

TIREE

Tobermory ●

TIREE   MULL

PERTHSHIRE

Glen
Orchy

ARGYLL

● Inveraray

Bannockburn ●
● Leith

GREAT SHEEP

Firth of Clyde

TWEEDDALE

Cheviot Hills

- - - County Boundary

21

landowner often gave the sheepman a warm welcome. He dreamed of having as fine a house as the landowners he was beginning to meet in Edinburgh or London, and of dressing and eating as richly as they did. He wanted higher rents from his land to be able to pay for these things. Sometimes he had tried already to encourage spinning, fishing or better farming and had made little money from it. But now the sheepmen were offering the money he needed. It was an offer which was difficult to resist and the blackfaced sheep began to march north. They covered many of the hills of northern Argyllshire, western Perthshire and southern Inverness-shire by the 1790s, when the parish ministers wrote reports for the 'Old Statistical Account of Scotland'. For example, the minister of Glenorchy wrote that:

> Numerous flocks of large and heavy sheep now graze almost the whole year on these mountains and wilds where before were to be found, and only for the summer months, a few light sheep and goats, small hill horses and some herds of black cattle. There may be about 20,000 sheep in the parish.

The typical sheep farm at this time would have about 2,000 sheep, looked after by two or three shepherds. (Later some were much larger.) The farm had to be large to make a big enough profit to pay the high rent. This was why few of the old tenants could afford to take up the new sheep farming. A great deal depended on the skill and hard work of the shepherds and their dogs. This was explained by Sir John Sinclair, one of the Highland landowners who knew most about sheep:

> An intelligent shepherd knows all his sheep from personal knowledge and can swear to their *identity*. The life of a shepherd, during summer, is not hard, but in a severe winter it is often dangerous. When snow drifts, he has to stay on the *windward* side of the hills with the sheep, in case they should be covered and suffocated.

The skill of the shepherd's dog has often been admired. While the shepherd stands in the valley, he sends his dog up the hill to drive the sheep to their new pasture. When the dog has done what he was told, he turns, looks at his master and waits further orders.

One of the nastiest tasks of the Highland shepherd was to smear the sheep every autumn. This was to protect the wool against maggots. Tar and butter were mixed together and rubbed into the fleece. It was a dirty job and took many days

A Highland shepherd.
This picture shows
clearly the plaid he is wearing
over his shoulder

to finish, but it had to be done until sheep began to be dipped in chemicals in the late nineteenth century. We can see how important the shepherd was by looking at the way he was paid. The usual method was that used in the 1790s around Fort William, where

> they each have a stone of oat-meal per week from the farmer, together with grass for 2 cows and 70 sheep, and they may plant as many potatoes for their own use as they can grow. They live very comfortably and generally save some money. Their sheep are marked for themselves and sold together with the master's and at the same price.

The shepherd would mix his own sheep among his master's and look after them together. Why do you think this suited his master?

By the 1790s the new type of sheep-farming was spreading further north, especially into the hilly country of Easter Ross around the Cromarty Firth and into Caithness. In 1792, 12,000 fleeces of wool were shorn in and around the parish of Kincardine, Ross-shire, where sheep had been brought in by the owner of the Balnagown estate, Sir John Lockhart Ross. Border sheep farmers were now hurrying north to Ross-shire to rent sheep runs.

CHEVIOT SHEEP

At about the same time at Langwell in Caithness a landowner was starting his own flock. He was Sir John Sinclair of Ulbster, a very keen farm improver. It was typical of Sir John that he ignored the blackfaced sheep, which had already been proved a success, and bought instead a flock of a new breed, the Cheviot. His example was followed by other sheepmasters, especially on the new sheep runs in Ross-shire. The Cheviot had first been bred on the Cheviot hills on the border between Scotland and England. It was longer than the blackfaced and its wool was of a higher quality. This was a great advantage in the 1790s, when fine wool was fetching higher prices than mutton. Unfortunately, the Cheviot was less hardy. One of the

Cheviot sheep

most famous sheepmen, Thomas Gillespie, tried both breeds on his farm near Fort William around 1800. He wrote:

> The Cheviot lambs are more tender than the blackfaced, particularly with heavy rains; and in unkindly springs the *ewes* have not so much milk to support their lambs as the blackfaced. The blackfaced are more active and better for their food on rocky, steep hills, and indeed the only reason to try the Cheviot kind is the wool.

As a result, both the blackfaced and the Cheviot were used, as sheep-farming spread gradually through the Highlands. Sheepmen continued to come from the borders and other parts of the Lowlands of Scotland to rent Highland hills. But sometimes (like Sir John Sinclair) the landowner would keep his own flock or let his land to a Highlander who could afford to pay a high enough rent. It was a colourful scene when these men came together for the yearly sheep and wool sales. One of the most important was the Inverness sale in July. This is what it looked like in 1837:

> Here you see the *portly* figure of a wool merchant of Huddersfield and Leeds; beside him the shrewd, broad-spoken

woollen manufacturer of Aberdeen or Bannockburn. The *burly* south-country *feeder* stands at the street corner in deep conversation, and about to strike a bargain with that sharp, red-haired little man, who is the largest farmer in the north and counts his flocks by 40,000 or 50,000. You may notice also from their military air the retired colonel and captain, who in the Highland regiments bled on the fields of Spain and Waterloo, and who now as sheep-farmers are passing the evening of their days in their native glens. Besides these there are small farmers, tall, stout, athletic fellows, some in kilts, with their plaids carelessly thrown over their shoulder. There also with their crooks are numerous common shepherds.

About 1,000 persons attend. The buyers know the stock of each farm and make their purchases without seeing either sheep or wool. They merely agree on a price and the time of delivery and payment. Bargains are thus said to be made at the market to the amount some years of £400,000. A casual observer would stare at this *motley* crowd of well-dressed people on the street, lounging from morning till night for two successive days, without any apparent purpose.

3   The Early Clearances

A landowner could become much richer if he brought in the sheepmen. His rents might rise by two or three times within twenty years. But what happened to the small tenant, his clansman, when the sheep marched on to the hills? At first he was often allowed to stay on in his old house and still grow his oats and potatoes in the *rigs* around the township. He would still keep his cattle and sell them to the drover every summer. But there was one important thing which now he could not do. About midsummer he had always taken his cattle away from the worn-out grazing round the township and up into the hills. There they would stay for about two months, eating the tender grass and growing fat enough to be sent to the autumn cattle sales. His family would move up to huts in the hills (called *shielings*) to look after the beasts. Often on dark and cold winter nights they would look forward to summer days at the shieling. This ended when the sheepmen came. The high pastures in the hills were now the home of the blackfaced sheep.

The Highlander and his family were sorry to miss their stay in the shieling but they were much more worried that their cattle would miss the summer grass in the hills. They now had to make do with the grazing around the township. It meant that fewer cattle could be kept. We have seen how important it was for the Highland tenant to sell cattle to earn money which he needed to buy oats and pay the rent. How could he keep his family fed if he had fewer cattle to sell? If he was lucky, he, his wife and his children might make some extra money by fishing, spinning or kelping, and the landowner might help them to do this. But, if he was unlucky, the tenant might get   27 no help or he might not earn enough by selling fish or thread or kelp. If so, he and his family might have to leave the township and try to find a living far away from the place they knew and perhaps even outside the Highlands. They had not been sent away by the landowner, but had decided that if they did not move they might starve.

After about 1780 many landowners began to realise that even more money could be made from sheep if they were allowed to graze in valleys as well as on the hills. But in the valleys were the farm townships where the small tenants lived and worked the land. Many landowners were unhappy about putting their clansmen off the land and out of their homes. Some refused to do it for many years. Others began to send away one or two families here and there to add small pieces of low ground to hill sheep walks. This was not enough for the Cheviot sheep. As we have seen, it was less hardy than the blackfaced. A Cheviot flock had to spend the winter on low and sheltered pastures. But the only land of this sort in the Highlands was already taken up by farm townships. This meant that, as the Cheviot was introduced from about 1790, it became more common for landowners to clear small tenants from large tracts of ground or even to empty an entire valley.

THE GLENGARRY CLEARANCES

Some of the largest of the early clearances were on the lands of Macdonell of Glengarry, which stretched from Loch Lochy to the west coast. As early as 1785 over 500 tenants were removed by their chief from the shores of Loch Quoich to make way for a sheep walk for Thomas Gillespie. They left peacefully, and marched sadly to Fort William, where they boarded the ship 'Macdonald' to make a new life in Canada. The next chief of Glengarry wanted to keep his clan around him. His name was Alistair Ranaldson Macdonell. He was a proud and bad-tempered man. He once quarrelled with an officer at a ball because they both wanted to dance with the same lady. He then killed the officer in a duel, was brought to trial and was very lucky to be found not guilty. He loved to organise Highland games where he could act as father of the clan in the old-fashioned way and watch what he thought were ancient highland sports. One visitor described what happened at the Glengarry games:

> The games were of the usual sort now common—dancing, piping, lifting a heavystone, throwing the hammer and running to Invergarry and back, six miles. One feat which I never saw since was twisting the four legs from a cow. At last one man succeeded. After struggling for about an hour, he managed to twist off the four legs. The *bard* of the clan who was present was then called out and told a poem in Gaelic in praise of the chief, his family and clan. The country people were all fed, dinner being laid out on the green—basins of broth, boiled and roast kelp and mutton, fowls, salmon, potatoes and a large quantity of oaten *bannocks*. There were no knives or forks, but the men's *dirks* and *skean dhus* were used to assist their fingers.

A race like the ones run at the Glengarry games

All this cost a great deal of money and the chief's debts rose rapidly. After 1802 he was forced to clear parts of Glengarry because he needed the high rents the sheepmen offered. He still wanted to keep his clan around him in the old-fashioned way and was angry when the people he cleared left for Canada. But, as he had given them nothing in place of the land they had lost, they had no choice.

THE DUKE OF ARGYLL

Many Highland landowners were shocked by what had happened in Glengarry and were determined that they would not treat their clansmen in this way. Some kept out the sheepmen. Some did lay out sheep walks, but spent a lot of time and

Inveraray Castle

money to find new work for the Highlanders on their estates. The 5th Duke of Argyll did this between 1770 and 1806. On the huge Argyll estates there were many sheep farms and their high rents helped to build a rich and handsome new castle at Inveraray, the ancient capital of the clan. But, unlike Glengarry, the Duke of Argyll encouraged new farming methods, spinning and fishing. He was Governor of the British Fisheries Society and he also set up a carpet factory near Inveraray. Although he did not always succeed, he worked hard to help the Highlanders make a living at home. This can be seen in orders he gave in 1771 to his *factor* on the island of Tiree:

> I am told that the island is over-peopled and my farms filled with a numerous set of poor tenants and cottars. I wish to relieve the farms of these people, and as I do not want to distress them I will help them to settle in a fishing village which I mean to set up in a suitable spot on the island.

THE ROSS-SHIRE SHEEP RIOTS

One of the surprising things is that when Highlanders saw sheep marching on to land which had been theirs, they usually accepted this without making a great fuss. The landowner might, like the Duke of Argyll, be trying to find them something else to do. Even if he did nothing, they were unused to resisting the orders of their chief. But in Easter Ross they did resist. On the last Sunday of July 1792 messengers waited at the church doors to call the men together on the banks of the river Oykel. Many answered the call, and they began to drive the sheep off the land, which had once been theirs, and over the hills into Inverness-shire. One man who watched thought they must have as many as 20,000 or 30,000 sheep. They were not thieves. We know this from an account by one of the officers of the regiment which was hurriedly called in to deal with them. He wrote that no one was hurt and the sheep only suffered from the long walk and the poor grazing on their journey. Not one sheep was killed, although the men were tired and hungry. The officer was very relieved that by the time the regiment 31 reached the scene the men of Ross had melted away into the hills. The soldiers did not want to have to open fire on them. Fifteen men from Strathrusdale were arrested and brought to Inverness to stand trial. Only six were found guilty, and before long they mysteriously escaped from prison and were never caught. It was clear that many people·sympathised with the men who had lost their land to make way for sheep.

EMIGRATION

Some people were particularly sorry that Highlanders were leaving their homeland to seek their fortune overseas, most often in Canada. They read of heartbreaking scenes as the *emigrants* sailed away, like the one illustrated here. A tall sailing ship would nose its way up a Highland loch and drop anchor off a village. Boats would bring out the emigrants, with their few belongings—a wooden trunk, an iron cooking pot and perhaps a dog. They would look sadly over the ship's rail at their relatives, standing wailing on the shore, and listen until the sounds faded away into the distance to a piper playing a lament, such as 'Lochaber no more'.

By no means all of these people had been forced out by sheep. Many simply found that, with more and more families scratching a living from the farm townships, they had to get out or run the risk of starving. Before 1800 there were never huge numbers of emigrants, but they had been trickling away ever since the 1750s. Some of the landowners were sorry to see them go. They still thought it was their duty to keep their clansmen round them. They also wanted to have plenty of people on their estates to man the factories and fishing stations they hoped might be set up.

THE DEVELOPMENT OF HIGHLAND TRANSPORT

It was because of these worries that, when the famous engineer Thomas Telford was sent by Parliament in 1801 to look at the

Opposite: *A nineteenth-century engraving of emigrants leaving the Highlands*

Highlands, one of his tasks was to see what could be done to stop people from emigrating. He reported in 1803 that about 3,000 people had gone away in the last year and that three times that number were likely to leave in the next year. His advice was that roads, bridges and a new canal should be built in the Highlands. These would provide work and, when they were finished, it would be easier to send fish and cloth and kelp south to be sold. This should give Highlanders a surer living for years to come. The Government agreed to these proposals and made Telford chief engineer of the scheme.

Every spring and autumn for over twenty years Telford made the long journey to the Highlands. During all that time the largest job he had to inspect was the Caledonian Canal. It was one of the engineering marvels of the age. It linked the east coast at Inverness with the west coast at Fort William by joining up three inland lochs. It meant that sailors no longer had to go round the north of Scotland through the fierce gales and tides of the Pentland Firth. There were serious engineering problems. You can read more about the building of the canal in another 'Then and There' book about Thomas Telford.

The canal was opened unfinished in 1822. It was not finally completed till 1847, by which time it had cost £1,300,000, about three times the original estimate. Despite this huge expense, it never carried nearly as much traffic as had been hoped.

Unlike the canal, Telford's roads and bridges in the Highlands have been well used. They can be seen on the map drawn up towards the end of the job by the body for which Telford built them, the Commissioners of Highland Roads and Bridges. They are still the main routes through the Highlands. There were great problems in carrying roads over mountain passes which were higher and moors which were wider than road-makers had ever tackled before. Roads and bridges were in danger of being carried away in bad weather. This is what

Opposite: *This map was drawn in 1828 for a report of the Commissioners of Highland Roads and Bridges. It shows the roads they had made or improved by that time*

happened in 1814 to Bonar Bridge, which links Ross-shire and Sutherland:

> A large number of fir logs, which had been rolled into the River Carron to be floated by the first flood, came down all together. Those logs which were upright struck the iron arch with such violence that the crash was heard at a considerable distance: but the bridge stood firm.

Some others were less fortunate. Despite these difficulties, 875 miles of roads and about 1,000 bridges were built in the Highlands by 1820 under Telford's control, at a cost of £454,000. They were good roads and have stood the test of many fierce winters. But they did not bring the factories and fishing stations which had been hoped. The markets of the south were still too far away. Telford and the 5th Duke of Argyll were only two of many men who tried to bring work to the Highlands. Unfortunately, they were not able to stop the mournful procession of Highlanders on to the emigrant ships or into the coal mines or cotton mills of the Scottish Lowlands.

4 The Sutherland Clearances

In July 1805 the *revenue cutter* 'Royal George' sailed from Leith on a mission which was to change the lives of thousands of people. She carried two important passengers. One was Elizabeth, Countess of Sutherland and Marchioness of Stafford. The other was her son George, Earl Gower, a student at Oxford University. On leaving the Firth of Forth, the 'Royal George' sailed north. The countess was determined to make the most of the cruise. She was a skilful artist and drew in a book many of the fine views she saw while sailing up the east coast of Scotland. Soon after she reached her destination, Dunrobin Castle, which was her house in Sutherland, she wrote a letter to her husband, the Marquis of Stafford, who was staying at home in England. She said she would send him the book of drawings. She also complained to him about the welcome given her at Dunrobin by the estate factor, Colonel David Campbell:

> His intention was that our servants should live upon Oat Cake and Whisky, and we were obliged to go without Bread ourselves at Dinner the day after we came because it was Sunday and he had only provided one Loaf, so we sent express to Tain for Bread. He never eats anything by himself but sour *whey* and Oat Cake to Dinner they say, and his housekeeper Miss Macintyre is the strangest old Skeleton you ever saw.

But this was much more than a holiday trip, and the countess was worried by more important things than the food at Dunrobin. When she was only one year old she had inherited an estate covering over half the huge county of Sutherland. She 37

A sketch made by the Countess of Sutherland of Dunrobin Castle in 1805

had not visited it very often since her marriage, but she and
her husband were now seriously concerned about the estate.
Was the amount collected from the rents as much as it ought
to be? Were the tenants getting a good enough living? In later
years it was said that the people of Sutherland had been very
content. For example, Angus McKay said that when he was a
boy in Strathnaver at about that time

> You would see a mile and a half between every town; there
> were four or five families in each of these towns, and bonnie
> *haughs* between the towns, and hill pasture for miles, as far
> as they could wish to go. The people had plenty of flocks of
> goats, sheep, horses and cattle, and they were living happy.

Elizabeth, Countess of Sutherland

They were remarkably comfortable—with flesh and fish and butter and cheese and potatoes and *kail* and milk too. There was no want of anything with them, and they had the Gospel preached to them at both ends of the *strath*.

A large number of people on the estate lived, like Angus McKay, in farm townships in the upland valleys or straths. But Angus told this to a parliamentary committee when he was an old man, nearly seventy years later. Had it really been like that? The people of the straths did often have a lot of animals. An account of Strathnaver, written at about the time Angus was a boy, says that each family had an average of 12 cattle, 6 small

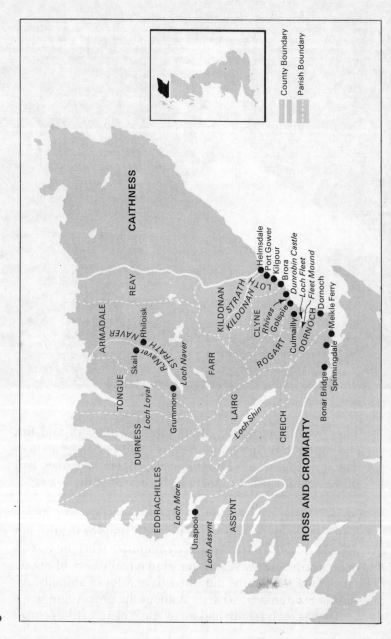

CAITHNESS

REAY

ARMADALE

DURNESS

TONGUE

Rhiloisk

Skail

Grummore

Loch Loyal

Loch Naver

R Naver STRATH NAVER

FARR

LAIRG

Loch Shin

EDDRACHILLES

Loch More

ASSYNT

Unapool

Loch Assynt

Helmsdale
Port Gower
Kilgour
Brora
Dunrobin Castle
Loch Fleet
Fleet Mound

KILDONAN

STRATH KILDONAN

CLYNE

Rhives

Golspie

ROGART

Culmailly

DORNOCH

Dornoch

Meikle Ferry

Spinningdale

Bonar Bridge

CREICH

ROSS AND CROMARTY

County Boundary
Parish Boundary

40

horses and 15 to 20 sheep. But it also says that the people could not grow more than half of the oats they needed on their tiny plots of *arable* land, and this was what they mainly lived on. Some people thought the small farmers were lazy and could do more to help themselves. For example, the minister of Rogart wrote that 'a poor tenant whose labour could well be spared from his little farm many days in the year will rather saunter or sit idle at home, than work for six pence a day, which would be a considerable addition to his own and his family's scanty meal'. He was right in saying that they did not have enough land to keep them busy all the time, but other work was difficult to find.

Like other landowners, the Countess of Sutherland also thought that sheep-farmers would have to be introduced to safeguard and increase the income of the estate. But, unlike Macdonald of Glengarry, she wanted to find a living elsewhere on the estate for the small tenants who were displaced and she was wealthy enough to try to do this. In 1803 the Duke of Bridgewater, who had made much of his fortune by building canals, had left the countess's husband an income which averaged £65,000 per year. The reason for the countess's visit to Sutherland in 1805 was to decide how some of this money could be spent to improve it. Although she still spent most of the year in England, she started coming to Sutherland most years for a stay of a month or two to enjoy a holiday.

She was joined at Dunrobin in July 1805 by her Edinburgh lawyers, Colin and William MacKenzie. Day after day they discussed with the factor, Colonel Campbell, what might be done. The countess wrote many letters to her husband to make sure he agreed. Finally a plan was hammered out. Some sheep farms would be set up in the hill country in the interior. Farm towns in the straths would have to be cleared to provide low winter grazing for the sheep. The people could move to villages to be built on the east coast at Helmsdale, Golspie and Kilgour. There they would be given *crofts* of moor land on which to grow oats or potatoes and a harbour to enable them to make

Opposite: *This map shows the interior of Sutherland from which people were cleared and some of the places on the coast to which they were moved*

money by fishing. The attraction of this plan was that it was expected to increase the income of the estate without harming the people in the farm townships. Colin MacKenzie, who was most keen about the plan, was worried that any attempt at sudden change 'would fail and only involve the bulk of the people in misery and ruin'. Changes in fact were even more gradual than he intended. One reason was that he fell ill in 1806 and never fully recovered. One sheep farm was formed in 1807 and two more in 1808. But one difficulty after another prevented the building of the fishing villages.

THE MEN FROM MORAY

New life was blown into the countess's plans by two energetic and ambitious men who arrived in Sutherland in 1809. They came from Morayshire. William Young had made his reputation by improving poor land along the seashore at Inverugie. He had drained and ploughed. He had built roads, canals and a fishing village at Hopeman. The villagers reaped a large harvest of crops and fish and so the village flourished. Now he was helping to start a regular sailing *packet service* from the nearby harbour at Burghead to Sutherland. On the first voyage, in July 1809, a young lawyer from Elgin went with him. His name was Patrick Sellar. They felt they were travelling to an exciting new country and they were not disappointed by what they found.

Young and Sellar saw in the east coast of Sutherland a country which, they were sure, not only needed a packet service, but would also pay rich profits to anyone who would improve the land in the same way as had been done in Morayshire. They took a *lease* of a 300-acre farm at Culmailly, near Golspie. They agreed with Colin MacKenzie that the small tenants should live in a village, where they could farm a croft of land reclaimed from the moor, but they would get the greater part of their living by fishing or by making linen or woollen cloth. It would cost the estate a lot of money. The people might not like being moved from ground their families had occupied for generations. In the end, however, everyone would be better off, if they were prepared to work. The countess was very impressed by these two men from Morayshire and thought they could make these ideas work. In 1811 Young became factor, with the job of carrying out his plans for the county. Patrick Sellar was to assist him.

THE KILDONAN RIOTS

At first it seemed that the people were willing to accept the plans made for them. There were clearances in 1812 in the parishes of Rogart, Loth, Clyne, Golspie and Assynt. The tenants moved off the land without making any trouble and the sheep moved in unhindered. But 1813 was very different. In January 1813 Gabriel Reid set out from Golspie to inspect the land he was to take over as a sheep farm in Strath Kildonan. He found himself the centre of a riot and he and his shepherds, who were already in the strath, were chased out. The men of Kildonan fought for many weeks to stay in their homes. William Young had offered them plots of ground on the north coast of the county on the estate of Armadale. It had just been bought by the countess to provide land for the people who were to be moved from the straths, but they did not believe it was good enough to give them a living.

On 2 February Patrick Sellar and the *sheriff-substitute* of the county rode up Strath Kildonan to persuade the people to sign a promise that they would keep the peace. They were met by 150 men who told them that 'they had the right to keep possession of their grounds and would allow no shepherd to come to the country'. They complained that the sheep farmers would ruin them and their families. This was a very serious matter for the estate managers. The law said that the land was the countess's to use as she wished. The people were 'tenants at will', who could be put off at any time. But the men of Kildonan claimed that the ground which their families had farmed for generations was theirs and that they had the right to stay. Such troubles would frighten off the sheep breeders and linen manufacturers from the south whose help was needed if the improvement plan for the estate was to succeed. Gabriel Reid, 43 whose visit to Kildonan had started the trouble, was certainly scared. Sellar wrote to the countess that 'Mr Reid is with us at present, and he is under very great, tho' I trust in part groundless, alarm for his personal safety. He is at the castle (Dunrobin) as a place of safety'. Worse was to follow. Several men who were thought to be the leaders of the rioters were summoned to appear at the sheriff court to be held at Golspie Inn on 10 February. They came, but not alone. James Duncan, the innkeeper, described what happened:

> About twelve o'clock a vast crowd of people from the parish of Kildonan assembled at my door, each of them armed with a *bludgeon*. The sheriff officer, who had a *warrant* for the arrest of the leaders, was prevented from arresting them by the crowd surrounding them and declaring that none of their number should be laid hold of for any purpose whatever. From the *temper of mind* in which the men appeared to be I did not think it safe for the officer to make the arrests even if he had a party of one hundred men. I saw a man of the name of Bruce put his left hand round one of the people whom the officer *apprehended* and pull him into the crowd, while with his right he brandished his stick above the officer's head.

No one was hurt, but what might happen next? Sellar, who was a courageous man, went among the Kildonan men as they were gathering at Golspie. He wrote to the countess that 'on my trying to point out the folly of a handful of men pretending to fight against the laws and strength of the British constitution, they said that they were loyal men whose brothers and sons were now fighting *Bonaparte* and that they would allow no sheep to come into the country'. If they did not allow the sheep in, the countess's plans for the estate would collapse. It was a moment of crisis, and she knew it.

The Kildonan people gathered together enough money to send a *petition* to the countess and her husband in London. It was carried by William Macdonald, who had been a recruiting sergeant and spoke good English. He was received in the

Kildonan Kirk and Strath. There are very few modern gravestones in the kirkyard. Why is this?

splendour of Cleveland House, the countess's London home, but the petition was rejected. Young was told to press ahead with the *evictions*. Troops would have to be used if the people were determined to resist. A powerful band of soldiers was brought from Fort George, near Inverness, accompanied by some artillery. When the soldiers arrived in Kildonan in March active resistance ended. The people did not accept all the plans made for them. So few agreed to move to Armadale that Young gave up the idea of settling any there. Seven hundred accepted an offer by the Earl of Selkirk to find land for them on the Red River in Canada, and by July 1813 more than a hundred had actually left for the New World. But the soldiers broke the Kildonan men's will to stop the advance of the sheep, and the evictions were carried out peacefully in May. Sellar was angry when, after being arrested, the leaders of the rioters were released. He wrote that 'I saw six of the ringleaders feasted in 45

Rhives parlour, Mr Young drawing ale for them'. (Rhives was the factor's house.) Young could afford to be kind. Many thousands of people were to be evicted from the Sutherland straths before there was another riot by tenants refusing to go.

The countess and her managers were convinced that they had broken resistance to their plans, and expected no serious trouble in 1814. At first events seemed to prove them right. A large sheep farm was to be set up in Strathnaver at Rhiloisk on the east bank of the river Naver. Patrick Sellar became tenant of the farm by offering a higher rent for it than his competitors. It was settled in December 1813 that Sellar would take over the farm in May 1814. Young planned to resettle the people who would have to be cleared from Rhiloisk on the north coast of the county. To make this easier he asked Sellar to move as few as possible in 1814. Sellar met the people of Rhiloisk in January 1814 and agreed that half of them could stay for another year. The other half would have to go in May. At the beginning of June they had still not moved. On 8 June Sellar began to turn them out, pulling down their houses to make sure they did not return. In doing this he was acting, not as under-factor of the estate, but as the new tenant of the farm. He had a legal warrant to evict the people. For them it was a bitter moment. Some of the families had lived there for as long as anyone could remember. Now they had to leave the land they knew and move very hurriedly with their belongings across about ten miles of rough country to a place which was strange to them. Seventy years later Angus McKay could still remember clearly what happened to him during the move:

> My father and mother and my brother went away, having got notice that if anything was upon the ground at twelve o'clock they would be fined. They rose in the morning and went away with the animals to the place they were to live in after, and left me and my brother who were younger sleeping in the bed; and there was a woman came and said,

'Won't you wake up, Sellar is burning at a place called Rhistog.' We got such a fright that we started out of bed and ran down to the river, because there was a friend of ours living on the other side. I took my brother on my back and through the river I went; and the water was that deep that when it came upon his back he began crying and shaking himself upon my back, and I fell, and he gripped round about my neck. We were both *greeting*, and took a fright that we would be drowned. There was a poor woman coming with her family up the strath, and she saw us and jumped into the river and swept us out of it.

Despite the misery of moving, the people did not refuse to go. There were no riots as there had been in Kildonan the year before. Young and Sellar sighed with relief, but their relief did not last long. In July 1814 a petition was sent to the countess by the evicted tenants of Rhiloisk. They made three complaints against Sellar. In March, two months before they were to go, his shepherds had burned all the *heath*, leaving no pasture for their cattle. Immediately they moved, he had pulled down the houses, barns and mills, although by custom the barns and mills should have been left for them to come back and harvest the crop which was in the ground. Thirdly, he had only allowed a few days for them to carry off their wood (which was in very short supply in Sutherland and which they needed to build their new houses), after which his shepherds had stopped them coming back.

The countess's answer was that, if they had any complaints against Sellar, they should take him to court, which they did. At first they only wanted money from him to cover their losses, but the matter became much more serious in 1815 when he was accused of actual crimes. The sheriff-substitute of the county, Robert MacKid, went to Strathnaver to collect evidence. In May 1815 he wrote to the countess's husband, Lord Stafford, to tell him that Sellar was guilty of a long list of crimes. As a result Sellar was arrested, locked up for a short time in the prison at Dornoch and brought to trial in April 1816. He was 47 charged with setting fire to the houses at Rhiloisk and causing the deaths of three people. Can we find out whether he was guilty of these crimes? Donald Macleod was a stonemason in Strathnaver. He watched the clearances in 1814, and was in no doubt of Sellar's guilt. Here is his description of what happened.

> When they had overthrown the houses in a large tract of country, they set fire to the wreck, so that timber, furniture and every other article that could not be instantly removed was consumed by the fire. In these scenes Mr Sellar was present, and apparently (as was sworn by several witnesses at his subsequent trial) ordering and directing the whole. Many deaths ensued from alarm, from fatigue, and cold; the people being instantly deprived of shelter, and left to the mercy of the weather. To these scenes I was an eye-witness. I was present at the pulling down and burning of the house of William Chisolm, in which was lying his wife's mother, an old bed-ridden woman of near 100 years of age, none of the family being present. I informed the persons about to set fire to the house of this, and prevailed on them to wait till Mr Sellar came. On his arrival I told him of the poor old woman being in a condition unfit for removal. He replied, 'Damn her, the old witch, she has lived too long; let her burn.' Fire was immediately set to the house, and the blankets in which she was carried were in flames before she could be got out. She was placed in a little shed; she died within five days.

Many people at the time supposed Sellar was guilty, as have many writers since. Sellar, on the other hand, claimed that he had not evicted anyone from houses where there were sick people. He denied burning any house, except that of William Chisolm, a tinker who did not belong to Strathnaver. He said that the other tenants had asked him to turn Chisolm out and to burn his house in case he tried to come back. He claimed it had not been burned until it was empty.

48   Which of these stories was nearer the truth? Sellar was able

to point out that in the original complaint of the tenants, made to the countess only a month after the evictions, there had been no talk of houses being burned or people dying. If these things had really happened, it is very surprising that the tenants complained only about less serious matters. The serious charges were first mentioned almost a year later, when sheriff-substitute MacKid began collecting evidence. However, there had been a quarrel between Sellar and MacKid for several years; according to Sellar, this was because MacKid enjoyed poaching, and Sellar had tried to stop him. There is certainly evidence that MacKid was unfair to Sellar. Although his legal duty was simply to find if there was a case to answer and to decide whether a trial should be held, he at once wrote to Lord Stafford suggesting that Sellar was guilty. He also told William Young that the people 'wished to see Sellar hanged or sent to Botany Bay' (a settlement in Australia to which criminals were sent). The tenants would naturally resent the evictions and bear a grudge against the man who had carried them out. Is it possible that, in their distress, they exaggerated the horrors of the evictions and that MacKid made the most of this evidence to try to destroy Sellar? If this was so, what of the account of Donald Macleod, who claimed to have seen Sellar committing these crimes? He wrote his account about twenty-five years later, after he himself had been evicted from the estate. This must at least make us wonder whether the details of his story are correct.

Sellar's trial was held in Inverness in April 1816. Everyone got very excited about it. People felt that the whole Sutherland plan was on trial. As was the custom at that time, the trial continued without a break until it was completed. It took thirteen hours. When at one o'clock in the morning the foreman of the jury at last announced the verdict of 'not guilty', Sellar was so tired and tense that he burst into tears. It has been suggested that the jury was *biased* and had been influenced by the Countess of Sutherland. It is certainly true that juries were then made up of men of property, who were not likely to be sympathetic to the evicted tenants. But the letters of the 49 countess and her advisers make it clear that they tried hard not to influence the verdict. If Sellar was found guilty they wanted to be able to say that he had not been acting in Strathnaver as under-factor but as tenant of the farm, and that therefore they were not involved. If, on the other hand, the verdict was 'not guilty', the last thing they wanted was for people to be able to say the jury had been bribed or threatened.

The countess and her advisers were sure that Sellar was not guilty of widespread house burning or of causing deaths, but they were unhappy about what he had done in Strathnaver. The countess complained that 'he is so exceedingly greedy and harsh with the people'. There is no doubt that he was hard and pushing and could be very rude. James Loch, adviser to the countess's husband, said that Sellar had 'a quick, sneering, biting way of saying things in carrying out his duty which I do not think has made him popular with anybody'. He despised the people of Sutherland and often referred to them as 'barbarians'. It is quite likely, therefore, that he enraged the families he evicted in 1814 by adding insult to injury. But William Young, the factor, thought that Sellar was at fault in another way. He complained that he was in too great a hurry to make profits from his sheep farm, and should have given the tenants much longer notice before clearing them off his land.

Sellar, however, was able to point out that Young was also at fault. One reason the tenants had been unwilling to move was that the *lots* they were to occupy on the coast were not marked out until two or three weeks after they were supposed to leave Rhiloisk. They were being expected to leave home for a completely unknown destination. This was Young's job and he should have done it sooner. There were other complaints about the new lands on the coast. Men who had their own plots of land at Rhiloisk found that on the coast they had a few strips scattered round an open field shared by many others. The countess began to think that, although Young had great plans for the estate, he was not good enough at the practical details of carrying them out. She was worried also by the enormous sums he was spending on other projects, like a coal pit at Brora and a mound to carry the road across Loch Fleet. The result was that Young lost his job on the estate in 1816 and Sellar lost his in 1817. The ambitious men from Moray had failed to give satisfaction.

THE CLEARANCES OF JAMES LOCH

The new factor was Francis Suther, but the man who was now really in charge of the Sutherland estate was James Loch (Lord Stafford's adviser), although he spent most of his time in England. Both Loch and the countess thought they should continue to move the people of the straths down to the coast and plans were made for widespread clearances to begin in 1819. But they were determined that this time there would be no cruelty and no mismanagement. People would be told well in advance exactly where they were to move to, and the officers carrying out the evictions would be careful not to lay themselves open to charges of the sort Patrick Sellar had faced.

The ruins of a cleared township at Achness, Strathnaver

In May 1819 about 700 families, amounting to between 3,000 and 4,000 people, were to be evicted from eight different parishes. Once again, the largest clearance was to be in Strathnaver, from a line of townships running ten miles down the west bank of the Naver from Grummore to Skail. On the final Sunday before the evictions many of these people gathered to worship together for the last time. The service was held in the open air. The minister, the Rev. Donald Sage, had prepared a sermon which he hoped would give his people courage, but before he could finish it he and his listeners broke down and cried.

In London Loch waited confidently for news. He was horrified to hear there had been burnings. Donald Macleod wrote later that at about eleven o'clock on the night of the Strathnaver clearance he climbed a hill and

> counted two hundred and fifty blazing houses, many of the owners of which were my relations, and all of whom I personally knew; but whose present condition, whether in or out of the flames, I could not tell. The fire lasted six days, till the whole of the dwellings were reduced to ashes or smoking ruins. During one of these days a boat lost her way in the dense smoke as she approached the shore; but at night she was enabled to reach a landing place by the light of the flames.

Perhaps he was using some imagination here, but many people who were in Strathnaver that day swore that the houses had been burned. The factor, Mr Suther, admitted to a very angry James Loch only that houses had been burned in Strathbrora. The people had said they would not leave. If he had merely pulled the houses down, they could have rebuilt them as soon as he and his men went away. The sheep farmers would then have been unable to bring in their animals. What else could he have done?

Clearances continued in Sutherland in 1820 and 1821, but it was difficult now for anyone to believe that the people had been persuaded that they were being evicted for their own good.

Their anger was only too clear. In the summer of 1819 more than 1,000 people attended great meetings held at the Meikle Ferry, near Dornoch, by an *agitator* called Thomas Dudgeon. He prepared a petition against the clearances to be sent to Parliament. In March 1821 the people of Achness, in the parish of Clyne, rioted when ordered to leave their land. Once again, as in Kildonan in 1813, soldiers had to be brought from Fort George to force them to go. When in June 1821 Loch reported that the programme of removals had been completed, he and the countess were relieved that it had been done without sparking off an armed rebellion in the county.

THE PLAN THAT FAILED

We do not know exactly how many people were cleared from their homes on the Sutherland estate, but between 1807 and 1821 the number must have been nearly 10,000. Few of the Highlanders understood why they were moved, because no one explained the reasons to them. All they knew was that they were forced to leave, often at short notice, the lands their families had farmed for generations, and that as they moved out an army of sheep marched in. The factors did not understand why the people hated moving so much and thought they were just lazy and old-fashioned and must be forced to obey. The countess also seems to have thought this. After the 1814 Strathnaver clearances she met the new minister of the parish and wrote to her husband:

> He says the people of Strathnaver are all settled comfortably and much to their advantage on their new crofts, and quite satisfied, and that the affair is much more thought of out of the country than in it, and that they are ready and willing to pay due attention to their rulers, but are misled to think we are on their side in this instance, which makes it the more necessary for us to let the real state of the case be known to them. Now the country is really becoming good for something, the people must be improved in order to suit it.

It is clear from this that the countess did not understand how her people felt. She spent most of her time 600 miles away in London, and even when she was in Sutherland she very rarely talked to them about her plans. As a result, they thought that she had preferred sheep to men in order to get higher rents. They did not forgive her, nor did their children or their grandchildren.

The countess was shocked and hurt when she realised that people thought her greedy and cruel. She said that she had wanted to give a better living to the people of the straths as well as to increase rents. We have seen that this was true. She also said that for years she had made no profit from the Sutherland estate. We can find out if this was true by looking at these figures, which show the money put into the estate by the countess and her husband and the money they took out of it in rents.

Money put into and taken out of the Sutherland estate, 1803–17

Year	£s put in	£s taken out
1803		5,872
1804		3,565
1805		3,899
1806		3,599
1807	1,261	4,394
1808	10,611	2,264
1809	1,813	2,800
1810	6,799	4,100
1811	799	4,070
1812	25,336	2,661
1813	45,302	1,375
1814	14,000	1,226
1815	8,539	2,327
1816	14,635	2,130
1817		1,650
Total	£129,095	£45,932

You can work out how much more was put into the estate than taken out of it between 1803 and 1817. How did all this spending help the people of Sutherland? It certainly helped many of them to make a living by fishing. Fishing stations were set up at Helmsdale, Brora and Port Gower. The money was used to build harbours, houses, storage sheds and curing yards, in which the fish were salted and put into barrels. Helmsdale for a time became a boom town. James Loch, when he visited it in 1819, wrote that it 'as usual was delightful, so full of life and increasing wealth, about 2,200 people hard at work tumbling over each other like ants'. But the boom did not last long. Fish prices dropped heavily in the 1820s. The fishermen still sailed out of the harbours the countess had built, but their numbers were no longer growing every season.

A modern photograph of the harbour built by the Countess of Sutherland at Helmsdale. The ruined building was a warehouse where the salted fish were stored

Perhaps the countess and her advisers expected too many people to be able to make a living from fishing and a tiny plot of land, but they did realise that other jobs would be needed. They planned that Brora would become a centre of industry. A coal mine was opened there at great expense. Some of the coal was used to heat salt pans, in which salt was boiled out of sea water. A brewery and a brick and tile works were built. Some of the people of the straths got jobs in these works, but not for long. Almost all prices were dropping after the end of the war with France in 1815, and the products of distant Sutherland had to be carried too far to their customers to be sold cheaply. The collapse of prices could not have come at a worse time for Sutherland. It meant that none of the projects into which the countess put money produced as many jobs as had been expected. It also meant that less money was earned by selling cattle, on which many small tenants on the estate still depended. Even some of the sheep farmers complained that they were not earning enough to pay their rent. As a result, Sutherland in the 1820s was not, as the countess had hoped, a land full of successful fishermen, busy industrial workers and prosperous small tenants. It was still a land of poverty, as it had always been. It was now also a land haunted by bitter memories of clearances and burnings.

5 Famine

There were many Highlanders in the army which defeated
Napoleon at the Battle of Waterloo in 1815. Some of them had
been soldiers for many years and they were now ready to come
home and settle down. Many were cruelly disappointed. They
found that times were hard in the Highlands and getting harder.
The price of kelp, which in 1810 had stood at over £20 per ton,
had dropped by 1815 to £10. By 1828 the best grades of kelp
sold at £4.15s. and by 1834 at £3. Now that the French no
longer ruled the continent of Europe, high quality soda could
once again be brought in from abroad. The makers of soap and
glass no longer depended on the seaweed gathered on highland
beaches. Gradually kelp gathering was abandoned, first on
the shores of the mainland and later in the Western Isles. The
price paid no longer covered the cost of gathering it and sending
it south. To make matters worse, cattle were also fetching much
lower prices. In 1810 a three-year-old was worth about £6, but
by the 1830s only about £3.10s.

In the years after 1815 the Highlander found it more and
more difficult to earn any money. The things he had sold for
cash (kelp and cattle) fetched less and less or even became
impossible to sell at all. How could he manage without this
money? He could grow more potatoes. A potato patch should
keep his family eating far longer than if the same piece of ground
was planted with oats. He would now plant potatoes on a much
larger part of the croft, and hope that this would allow him to
do without the extra oats he usually had to buy from the
merchant in Inverness or Greenock. What made this difficult
was that the population was still increasing, especially in the

57

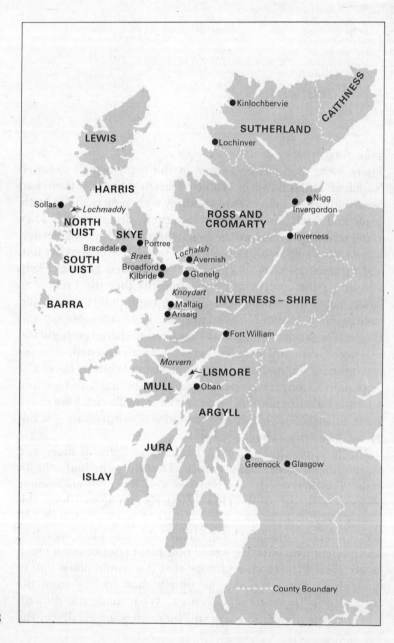

Kinlochbervie

SUTHERLAND

CAITHNESS

LEWIS

Lochinver

HARRIS

Nigg
Invergordon

Sollas ● Lochmaddy

ROSS AND
CROMARTY

NORTH
UIST

SKYE

Inverness

Bracadale ● Portree

SOUTH
UIST

Braes

Lochalsh

Avernish

Broadford

Glenelg

Kilbride

BARRA

Knoydart

INVERNESS – SHIRE

Mallaig

Arisaig

Fort William

Morvern

LISMORE

MULL

Oban

ARGYLL

JURA

ISLAY

Greenock ● Glasgow

- - - County Boundary

north-west Highlands, so the small tenant probably had more mouths to feed. If he still had to buy oats, how could he find the money to pay the rent? Often he could not, and his rent fell further and further into *arrears*.

Soon some landowners were in trouble. They could not collect anything like the amount of rent due, but they still had to keep their families and servants and their houses in the Highlands and perhaps in Edinburgh or London. Many had also to pay interest each year on their debts, which were often large. What were they to do? Some decided that they must either clear off small tenants who could not pay rent and bring in sheep farmers who would pay it regularly, or sell the land to Lowlanders or Englishmen and leave it to them to bring in the sheep. If they did not do one thing or the other, they were afraid they would go bankrupt. As a result, the blackfaced and Cheviot sheep marched in the 1820s and 1830s on to many new pastures.

One of the places where this happened was the Glenmorvern estate on the Morvern peninsula in Argyllshire. It was sold in 1824 by the Duke of Argyll to a wealthy Edinburgh lady, Miss Stewart, who made it into two sheep farms. One of the townships which had to be cleared was Unimore. Mary Cameron lived at Unimore and described later how she left it:

> The day of the *flitting* came. The officers of the law came along with it, and the shelter of a house, even for one night more, was not to be got. It was necessary to depart. The hissing of the fire on the hearth as they were drowning it reached my heart. We could not get even a *bothy* in the country; therefore we had nothing for it but to face the land of strangers [the Lowlands]. The aged woman, the mother of my husband, was then alive, weak and lame. James carried her on his back in a *creel*. I followed him with little John and Donald. Our neighbours carried the little furniture that remained to us, and showed every kindness which friendship could show.

Opposite: *This map shows the areas of the later clearances*

On the day of our leaving Unimore, I thought my heart would break. We sat for a time on the Hill of Cairns to take the last look at the place where we had been brought up. The houses were being already stripped. The bleat of the 'big sheep' was on the mountain. The whistle of the Lowland shepherd and the bark of his dogs were on the *brae*.

We reached Glasgow and through the minister's letter we got into a cotton work [factory].

Some landowners, although they were short of money, were most unwilling to allow this to happen to their tenants. They still thought, like the clan chiefs of the past, that it was their duty to keep their people around them. Lord Macdonald was one landowner who thought this. He and his advisers tried hard to convince themselves that clearances and emigration were not the answer. A report made to him about his Skye estate in 1829 said this:

That there is an *excess* of population on the estate and that the removal of many would be in the interests of all is most obvious. But it unfortunately happens that when an emigration does take place the best of the tenants, those who have means, are among the first to emigrate, leaving merely the scum behind, a class of people wholly unable to stock land [with cattle]. I think that, once the whole estate has been carefully inspected, and it has been fully and fairly worked out what each piece of land can truly pay, and the rents adjusted accordingly, then matters will go on smoothly and pleasantly.

But for a landowner to try to avoid clearances was a dangerous gamble. Often matters did not go on smoothly and pleasantly. By the early 1850s Lord Macdonald's debts were so large that he had to hand over control of his estate to *trustees*. Their job was to make enough money from it to pay off the men from

Opposite: *A drawing of Godfrey William Wentworth, 4th Lord Macdonald, made in 1845*

whom he had borrowed, and they did this by carrying out the clearances he had tried for so long to prevent.

Another landowner who was determined not to send his people away was Macdonald of Clanranald. To keep his clansmen on his estate on the island of South Uist, he gave them oatmeal when their own supply ran out and sometimes money to buy a new horse or cow if they had lost one. His factor proudly claimed that in every difficulty the crofters came to him for help and advice and were rarely disappointed. But the only way this could be paid for was by selling off bits of land. This began in the 1820s and by 1838 Clanranald had lost the entire South Uist estate.

Clanranald and Lord Macdonald were not unusual. Many clan chiefs lost their land in the same way. Most of them were known personally to Joseph Mitchell, whose work as an engineer took him among them often in the fifty years after 1820. Looking back at the end of his life, he realised that 'I have seen nearly two thirds of the estates in the Highlands in my time change *proprietors*'.

THE POTATO FAMINE, 1846

In many parts of the West Highlands it was difficult for a man to feed his family even when the potatoes were healthy and sweet. But in 1845 came news from Ireland that potatoes were withering overnight and turning black. Soon there were reports of the same thing happening in the Scottish borders. Throughout the Highlands people went out at first light every morning to look at their fields, praying that they would escape the potato blight. For a while they did, but in the autumn of 1846 it struck. The 'Inverness Courier' reported:

A friend had a few days ago gone to Knoydart, Skye, Lochalsh and Kintail, and he tells me that in all that extensive district he had scarcely seen one field which was not affected. Unless a gracious *Providence* look upon our poor Highlanders in mercy there is every likelihood that starvation must be their portion.

It was soon clear that the potato crop had failed in all parts of the Highlands. The same thing happened in the following year, 1847, and the effects continued to be felt for long after that. What would happen to the people, especially on the West Coast and in the Islands, who had come to depend on the potato? Many landowners helped their tenants by giving them oatmeal or money in return for building dykes or other work around the estate. One who did this was Macleod of Dunvegan in Skye. It was said to be costing him from £175 to £225 a week, and when he was told that he could not afford it, he replied that 'ruin must be faced rather than let the people die'. But the blight had been so general and the need was so great that the landowners could not give enough for everyone. It was from the *manse* of Bracadale, part of Macleod's estate, that the Rev. Norman Mackinnon wrote in December 1846 that the people were

> now in actual want of everything in the shape of food; some of them days past told me that they had not eaten anything for two days but a salt herring which they said 'kept them in good heart'. This day a great number of them came to my house, who said that they had not a bite and the meal store was run out; a Government store-ship having come into the loch on her way to Portree, they thought I could get them to land some of it, but this could not be done. Oh, send us something immediately. If you can send but a few pounds at present, let it come, for many are dying, I may say, of starvation.

Mr Mackinnon was writing to the Secretary of the Highland Relief Board. This had been hurriedly set up to collect money from people in the Lowlands and England who were shocked to hear about the potato famine and who wanted to help the Highlanders. The Board sent north many cargoes of oatmeal. It thought that those who wanted meal should do some work for it if they were able and they were often set to work to build piers or roads. In several parts of the Highlands the local people will still point out to you the '*destitution* roads' which were built during the famine years of the late 1840s. Highlanders who lived through these years remembered them vividly till the end of their days. Duncan McDonald of the island of Lismore recalled thirty-five years later that

> I have seen some of these people who formerly had crops and cattle, and butter and cheese, and milk afterwards, in those years going with their barley *scone* to a good well which was beside us and take their meal—barley and water—and it grieved me sorely.

He also remembered changes the landowner had made during the years of the potato famine.

> The property consisted of six or seven townships. There have been over 400 or 500 souls there, and over the whole tract now there are only three shepherds and a manager. He was sending us away one after the other, and he himself gathering stock which he placed upon every place as it became vacant.

THE GREAT EMIGRATION: 1840s AND 1850s

Many landowners, like the one on Lismore, decided that this new disaster meant they could no longer afford to keep a large number of small tenants on their estate. Because of the potato blight, many tenants were unable to pay their rent. Often the owner of the land had to supply them with oatmeal. He might bear the cost of this for one year or even two, as he had probably done in bad times in the past. But in the late 1840s far more crofters than ever before came to the factor to say that they could not pay the *laird*, and that in fact they needed his meal if they were not to starve. And on many estates this now seemed to be continuing, without hope of relief, year after year. Often a landowner who had supported crofters through lean years in the past now at last gave up hope of them ever being able to pay their way and decided that he had no choice but to move them out and bring in sheep. If he did not, he might suffer the

Opposite: *Skye crofters grinding oatmeal. Their black house is in the background*

same fate as Macdonald of Clanranald and lose his estate. The Cheviot and the blackfaced sheep marched over many more hills and valleys as a result of the potato famine, especially along the west coast of the Highlands and in the Western Isles.

But, if sheep were brought in to make sure that the laird got some income from his land, what was to become of the crofters? Sometimes they were sent away without anything being done to find them a new living. Sometimes they were given little plots of rocky or marshy ground on the estate which in the past they would not have thought worth ploughing. Both these things happened at Avernish, in the Balmacara district of Wester Ross. This is what it was like by 1883:

> The first three crofters have between them about twenty acres in all, including rocks, bogs and some fertile soil. They each keep two cows, and sow about one quarter oats, which on an average yields about double that quantity, and they have to sow very thick, owing to the poverty of the soil. Each plants about five barrels of potatoes, and the return averages twenty-four barrels. The remaining five crofters have fifteen acres between them.
>
> This was at one time an important township, and used to contain a large, prosperous, happy and contented population, but thirty-four years ago [1849] the bulk of the people were sent away by the factor, who wished to form a sheep farm for his son. Those who were allowed by the proprietor to remain after the factor had told them 'Go you must, even though you should go to the bottom of the sea', were allowed a mere fringe of the township, bordering on the rocky sea-shore.

Often, as at Avernish, the crofters blamed the factor, because he was the one who came to the township to put them out. Often, as at Avernish, crofters were moved to poor plots of land on the shore. Then the landowner could say that he had given a new living to some of his people. It might be so poor that after a while a number of the tenants would give up the struggle to make a living from it, and move off to find work in the

Lochcarron, a village on the coast built to house people from better land inland

Lowlands. There were other landowners who thought it was unfair to give a man a croft they knew could not feed a family and who were unhappy to think of crofters looking for a job in cotton mills, iron works and coal mines in the Lowlands. They thought it would be better for their people to make a new life in North America or Australia, where they could continue to be farmers and ought to be able to get a piece of good land. Many landowners were prepared to pay the cost if their tenants wanted to emigrate. Glenelg in Inverness-shire was one place from which a lot of people emigrated to Canada. One of the men who was able to stay in the glen was questioned during a 67

Government enquiry in 1883 about those who had gone:

Q. When did these people go away?

A. Upwards of thirty-four years ago.

Q. Did they go of their own accord, or were they sent away?

A. They went voluntarily. Some of them after getting on board the ship went ashore again, not wishing to go; but they were not allowed to remain, and their houses were pulled down over their heads, and they were forced to embark again.

Q. Were they assisted to go away?

A. They got their passage; Mr Baillie, the proprietor, paid for their passage.

Mr Baillie did ask for volunteers who wanted to emigrate, but he was so desperate to see them go that he would not let them change their minds and stay. His was not the only estate on which crofters had second thoughts about going to Canada. This happened also on Lord Macdonald's estate on the island of North Uist. We have seen that he tried hard for many years to avoid clearing his tenants off the land. But in the Sollas district the potato crop failed badly for several years running in the late 1840s. Lord Macdonald gave oatmeal to around 600 people there; so did the Highland Relief Board. Seeing that even with this help they could barely keep themselves alive he sent his factor, Mr Cooper, to Sollas to offer them a passage to Canada. When Mr Cooper first came to Sollas in March 1849 the people accepted the offer, but by the time he returned in July to see them off their land and on to the ships they had changed their minds and refused to go. They had known no place except their own island, and as the leaving day came near, they decided it was better to live, and if necessary die, there than to make a dangerous voyage to a strange land of which they knew nothing.

By this time Lord Macdonald's own position was desperate. He owed about £200,000 and, because of the potato famine, could not pay the interest on his debt. The men from whom he had borrowed were becoming more and more threatening.

The paddle steamer, 'Cygnet', which was chartered to take policemen to Lochmaddy in 1849

He decided that the people of Sollas must emigrate, whether they liked it or not. Sheriff-Substitute Colquhoun and thirty-four policemen came from Inverness to evict them. A reporter of the 'Inverness Courier' sailed with the police on the little steamer 'Cygnet', which was specially chartered to take them from the mainland port of Oban to Lochmaddy on North Uist. The man from the 'Courier' did not enjoy the voyage through the 'short, *crabbed*, punching sea that rolls continually through the Minch', but he recovered enough to write a full account of what happened at Sollas. He managed to interview the crofters on 1 August, which was spent in discussions between them and the factor. They told the reporter of their hardships and insisted that they would be able to pay rent if only they were given crofts of double the present size. But where was the land to come from? The following day the police moved in to force the people out. The reporter was there taking notes:

One woman threw herself upon the ground and fell into hysterics, uttering the most *doleful* sounds, and barking and

yelling like a dog for about ten minutes. Another, with many tears, sobs and groans put up a petition to the Sheriff that they would leave the roof over part of her house, where she had a loom with cloth in it, which she was weaving; and a third woman, the eldest of the family, made an attack with a stick on an officer and, missing him, she sprang upon him and knocked off his hat. So violently did this old woman behave that two stout policemen had great difficulty in carrying her outside the door.

The police were forcing the crofters to leave their houses, which were then thrown down by men brought from another part of the island. A crowd of Sollas people gathered and started shouting at them. At one house the furniture was thrown outside, the cloth was cut out of the loom on which the housewife had woven it, and then she rushed to the door with a baby in her arms shouting 'my children are to be murdered'. The crowd began throwing volleys of stones at the police, who had to form up in two lines and charge before the work could go on. There were cuts and bruises on both sides. After a few more families had been evicted, the excitement grew even stronger. The factor realised that, even if they were all forced out of their houses and their houses thrown down, they would still refuse to leave the area. So he admitted defeat and agreed that the people could stay till the following spring. Some in fact were allowed to stay at Sollas for good. Others moved the following year (1850) to new crofts on a barren moor in another part of the island, but these crofts were so poor that many of them emigrated to Australia in 1851.

Sollas was one of the few places in the Highlands where crofters resisted by force the men who came to evict them. Once more we find that in most places they gave in without a fight. Because of this it is difficult to work out how often it was the landowner who forced them to go. In later years Highlanders told many stories of the way lairds had thrown crofters

Opposite: *A girl carrying something heavy, probably manure to spread on the fields. Women did a lot of the heavy work around the croft*

71

out of their houses and driven them against their will on to ships which would take them to Canada or Australia. Some of these stories are certainly true. But often, during the potato famine and the years which followed, crofters left home, not because they had been told to go, but because they thought they would starve if they stayed. They set off for the smoky towns of the Lowlands or the backwoods of Canada because that seemed to be the only way of feeding their families. How many went for this reason only and how many were actually evicted it is impossible to say. What is certain is that many left home and never returned.

We saw that the number of people in the Highlands was rising till about the 1830s, but after that it began to drop. The number living in the four Highland counties (Argyll, Inverness, Ross and Cromarty and Sutherland) dropped by one-ninth in the forty years after 1841. This may not seem a great difference, but look at these figures, which show how many people lived in some of the parishes you have been reading about in this chapter.

	1841	1881
Bracadale	1,824	929
Glenelg	2,729	1,601
Lismore and Appin	4,193	3,433
Lochalsh	2,597	2,050
Morvern	1,781	828
North Uist	4,428	4,264

You will see that in some places the number of people did not drop very much, but in other places there were only about half as many people in 1881 as forty years earlier. Can you imagine what it would be like if half the people in your area disappeared? There had been clearances in the Highlands before the 1840s, but it was only from about then that huge numbers of Highlanders had to leave. They left grieving for the places where they, and their fathers before them, had lived for so long. This touched the heart of a Lowlander, Archibald Geikie, who was on holiday in Skye in 1851 when he saw emigrants marching from Suisnish to the ship which was to take them to Canada.

As I was returning from my ramble, a strange wailing sound reached my ears at intervals on the breeze from the west. On gaining the top of a hill, I could see a long and motley procession wending its way along the road that led from Suisnish. It halted at the point in the road opposite the manse of Kilbride, and there the *lamentation* became long and loud.

As I drew nearer, I could see that the minister, with his wife and daughters, had come out to meet the people, and bid them all farewell. Every one was in tears, each wished to clasp the hands that had so often befriended them; and it seemed as if they could not tear themselves away. When they set off once more, a cry of grief went up to heaven; the long plaintive wail, like a funeral *coronach*, was resumed; and, after the last of the emigrants had disappeared behind the hill, the sound seemed to re-echo through the whole wide valley of Strath in one prolonged note of desolation.

6 The Crofters' War

We have seen that many Highland chiefs lost their land in the mid-nineteenth century because their debts became so large. Often the new owners were wealthy Englishmen, who bought a Highland estate to use as a holiday home. Usually they would escape in August from the heat, dust and hurry of London or Birmingham and come north for a stay of two or three months. They would spend their holiday walking, fishing, shooting grouse or, most popular of all, stalking deer. Miss Conny Astley was a guest on the Ardtornish estate in Morvern in 1873. She described in her diary how she and her host were out on the hill looking for deer and heard the roaring of a stag.

> Suddenly a deep and awful sound is heard from the flat sort of strath which stretches between them and the stag. It sends a thrill of excitement through them and the *six-pointer* suddenly pauses and listens. They creep a little further forward and behold the Big Stag. For a full hour and a half they lie on the hill enjoying the exciting spectacle.

The stag was lucky that on this day they were not carrying their guns. Deer hunting became so popular that by the 1860s many acres of land in the Highlands were being set aside as deer forests. Sometimes crofters had to be cleared off the land to make way for deer. An Arisaig man remembered in 1883 that the deer forest near him was 'once land flowing with milk and honey, which supported scores of families in comfort, but

Opposite above: *Deer stalking in the Highlands*

Opposite below: *People being evicted from their homes, probably in Morvern*

75

who, alas! are now on account of the *mania* for sport scattered over the wide world'. In other places sheep runs were turned into deer forests. Sheep were not as profitable as in earlier years. Their price fell gradually from the 1870s because cargoes of Australian wool and New Zealand mutton were now reaching Britain. Also, some Highland sheep farmers had grazed too many sheep on their land and had tired out the hill pastures. Some landowners decided they could get higher rents by letting the hills as deer forests to wealthy Englishmen who did not have a Highland estate of their own. Unfortunately, a deer forest needed even fewer men to look after it than a sheep run. A shepherd complained in 1883:

> I am able to prove that the Lochalsh forest is laboured by one gamekeeper, and when under sheep there were four shepherds, three wintering shepherds, and several helpers, besides clipping and *smearing*. And then how can any man tell me that there is as much labour attached to deer forests as sheep walks? Now, if the people get the land, they will serve towns with beef and mutton, and supply themselves with the fat of the grass as in other days. But landlords today want nothing but a purseful of money, and that makes them let their hill and glens under deer instead of brave and powerful men, who would rise shoulder to shoulder to serve their Queen and country if required.

In fact, despite the deer forests, the owners of Highland estates rarely made a profit from them in the late nineteenth century. Because of this, many of them wanted to get higher rents from the crofters who still lived on their land and to make sure that the rents were paid regularly. Crofters were often sent letters like this by the factor:

To Mr Finlay MacInnes,
16 Waterloo, Tormore, by Broadford, Skye.
31st October 1872.

Sir, I have to *intimate* that your land and grazings have been valued at £1.15s, and you are to be charged at that rate from

Whitsunday last. If you consider yourself *aggrieved*, you will intimate the same to me, by writing, within ten days from this date, when I will relieve you of your lands and let to another.

Your obedient servant,
D. Macdonald.

N.B. I have strict orders to allow no arrears after Whitsunday 1873.

Now the crofters began to change. For about a hundred years they had usually accepted eviction without rebelling. But now they became more and more angry when they saw so much land being turned into deer forest, and when families which still had crofts were forced to pay higher rents or leave. Finally in 1882 they began to resist the landlords in what came to be known as 'The Crofters' War'.

The most serious trouble was in Skye. Lord Macdonald's tenants in the parish of Braes sent their cattle, against his orders, on to the pastures of Benlee, which had been taken away from them. He decided to make an example of about twenty of them by threatening to evict them and demanding that they give him all the rent they had failed to pay. The people of Braes decided to prevent this. The officer who came to give them legal warning was waylaid and the *summonses* he was carrying were burned. To help the local police forty-eight members of the Glasgow force were brought to Skye. They set out from Portree on a cold grey morning in April 1882 to march the eight miles to Braes and arrest the Highlanders. They took the crofters by surprise and managed to catch five wanted men, but soon a large crowd surrounded them, shouting and throwing stones. A newspaper reporter had come to see what happened. Here are some of the things he told his readers:

When the police drew their batons and charged, this was the signal for a general attack. Huge boulders darkened the horizon as they sped from the hands of infuriated men and women. Large sticks and *flails* were brandished and brought down with crushing force upon the police. The police were

ordered to run at the double for the pass which led to Portree. Would they manage to run through? Yes! No! On went the blue coats, but their progress was soon checked, stones were coming down like hail, while huge boulders were hurled down before which nothing could stand. Here and there a constable might be seen actually bending under the pressure of a well-directed rounder, losing his footing, and rolling down the hill. By keeping up the rush, the party got through the *defile* and emerged triumphantly on the Portree side.

It is surprising that no one was killed in what came to be called 'the Battle of the Braes', but many on both sides were bruised and cut. Throughout the Highlands crofters joined branches of the Highland Land League and held meetings to protest about the way they had been treated. Parliament appointed a *commission*, led by Lord Napier, which toured the Highlands in 1883 and asked the people about their grievances. What they wanted was plainly said by an old man in Morvern who had lost his croft. He told the commission: 'I would like to be the way I was before, if it were possible; that is I should like to have a croft and my cows back again as before.'

But it was not possible. There was no chance that Highlanders who had lost their crofts could be given them back. There were too many people in the Highlands and not enough good land. What Parliament did do as a result of the Napier Commission's report was to pass the Crofters' Holdings Act in 1886. This made important promises to people who still had crofts. At last, after over a hundred years of clearances by the landowners, they were given the right to remain on their crofts as long as they paid the rent. And a Crofters' Commission was given power to reduce rents, if it thought them unfair, and cancel

Opposite: *Between 1882 and 1884 the crofters of the Glendale and Kilmuir estates in Skye refused to pay rents, took over some sheep farms for the use of their own animals and kept the police out of the area. In this picture you can see the men of Glendale meeting in church to discuss the situation. Eventually in November 1884, a party of 300 marines was landed in Skye to restore order and stayed for seven months. But the crofters still refused to pay their rents*

Skye crofters at work planting potatoes in the 1880s. They are using seaweed instead of manure and are ploughing with a special spade called the cas chrom

arrears of rent. This was an important victory for the crofter. Ever since it has been almost impossible for a landowner to evict him. Rents were eventually reduced by about a quarter and crofters were excused from paying most of the arrears of rent they owed.

But in 1886 the protests continued. The Crofters' Commission took a long time to travel round the Highlands and announce its decisions. And the cottars, people who had already lost their crofts and who were always in danger of starving, knew that it could do nothing for them. In 1887 hundreds of cottars on the island of Lewis joined in a deer drive, in which they killed as many deer as they could before troops arrived from the south. In many places there were raids to seize for crofting land which was used only for sheep or deer. Gunboats had to be sent to

Police and soldiers facing land raiders in Lewis, 1888. The man in front of the troops is reading the Riot Act to the raiders

the west coast of Sutherland. It was not until 1888 that the protests died down and 'The Crofters' War' came to an end. These protests had persuaded Parliament to take special action to help the Highland crofter, which it has continued to do ever since.

7 Beyond Mountain and Sea

Where did the people go who had to leave the Highlands and make a new life somewhere else? Many went to the nearest place they could find work, the Lowlands of Scotland, and especially the area around Glasgow. It was easy to get to Glasgow from the West Highlands by boarding one of the steamboats which by the 1830s and 1840s were sailing regularly to all the more important places on the west coast. When a family came ashore at Glasgow's Broomielaw quay, they were not really in a land of strangers because so many Highlanders were there already. They might go to the Gaelic church on Sundays, hear a service in their own language and perhaps meet people who had come from home. They could be near friends and they could also get work. Many found jobs in huge cotton mills which were only a few hundred yards from where they had left the steamer. Others were taken on by iron works, coal mines, shipyards, engineering shops, railways and a host of other businesses. By the 1850s the area around Glasgow was becoming one of the greatest centres of industry in the greatest industrial nation in the world. It needed a constant stream of new workers.

Some of the Highlanders who went to Glasgow did well. They got steady work, perhaps even became a foreman in the factory or saved enough to start their own grocery store or public house or workshop. Others were less fortunate. They might lose one job after another or fall sick. Then they would have to live in the sort of slum houses illustrated here. A doctor described a

Opposite: *The slums of Glasgow in the 1860s*

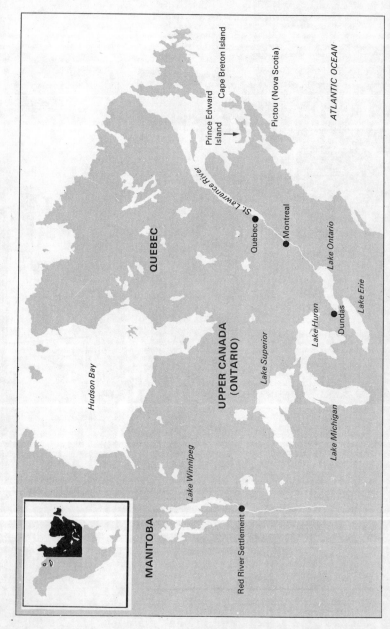

ATLANTIC OCEAN

Cape Breton Island

Pictou (Nova Scotia)

Prince Edward Island

St. Lawrence River

QUEBEC

Quebec

Montreal

Lake Ontario

Lake Erie

Lake Huron

Dundas

Lake Superior

UPPER CANADA
(ONTARIO)

Lake Michigan

Hudson Bay

Lake Winnipeg

Red River Settlement

MANITOBA

visit to houses like this in the 1840s:

> We entered a dirty low passage like a house door, which led
> through the first house to a court immediately behind,
> which court, apart from a narrow path around it, was
> occupied entirely by a dunghill of the most disgusting kind.
> There were no *privies* or drains there, and the dungheaps
> received all filth which the swarm of wretched inhabitants
> could give. Inside the houses we saw half-dressed wretches
> crowding together to be warm, and in one bed, although
> in the middle of the day, several women were imprisoned
> under a blanket, because as many others, who had on their
> backs all the articles of dress that belonged to the party,
> were then out of doors.

Some Highlanders could not bear the thought of living in a
town and working indoors. They wanted to continue as farmers.
If there was no longer enough land for them in the Highlands,
they would emigrate. Most of them went to Canada. Until
about the 1820s the most popular places to go to were on the
east coast of Canada, for example, Pictou (Nova Scotia), Cape
Breton and Prince Edward Island.

The first task of the new settler there was to cut down the
dense forest. He had to keep his axe swinging until he had
cleared enough space for his cabin and his fields. He used the
straightest trees to build his cabin and piled the rest in great
heaps, burned it and used the ash to fertilise the soil. One
settler in Nova Scotia wrote a poem in Gaelic, making this
complaint:

> Before I make a clearing and raise crops and tear the
> forest up from its roots by the strength of my arms, I'll be
> worn out, and almost spent before my children grow up.
> Piling tree trunks on top of each other in bonfires has
> strained every muscle in my back, and every part of me is
> so black that I'm just like soot.

Opposite: *This map shows some of the places in Canada where Highlanders settled*   85

Once this hard work had been done, good crops could usually be grown in the forest clearings. And the settler could often get a good meal by hunting or fishing. In Cape Breton lobsters could be picked up by hand from beaches all along the coast. *Moose* could be trapped in dozens by driving them into deep snow, where they could not move quickly. But not every new settler managed to feed his family. If he was too slow in clearing the forest, or if the fierce winter weather spoiled his crops, he might have to give up and move on. Many families who had to do this, and most new settlers from the 1820s, went further inland to Upper Canada (which is now called Ontario), or to Quebec or further still into Manitoba.

It was in 1812 on the Red River in what was to become Manitoba that the Earl of Selkirk began one of his settlements. We have seen that he was keen that Highlanders should come to Canada and that he persuaded some of the people evicted from the straths of Sutherland to follow him. The men of Kildonan named their part of the Red River after their old home. This was lawless country, and the Earl of Selkirk's settlers were twice driven out by their enemies. These enemies were not the Indians (who were friendly), but other settlers, some of them Scots. But the Red River Settlement survived. A more common problem for later settlers, especially in the late 1840s and the 1850s after the potato famine in the Highlands, was that they arrived, often at the beginning of winter, without enough money to buy land or even to get enough food until they could find a job. A newspaper in Upper Canada in 1851 wrote about this and explained why it was difficult for them to find work.

We have been pained beyond measure for some time past to see in our streets so many unfortunate Highland emigrants, apparently destitute. Their last shilling is spent probably before they reach the upper province—they are reduced to begging. Their case is made worse by their ignorance of the English tongue. Of the hundreds of Highlanders in and around Dundas at present perhaps not half a dozen understand anything but Gaelic. We may assist these poor creatures for a time, but charity will not keep so many for a very long period. Winter is approaching, and then—but we will leave this painful subject for the present.

Despite these problems, many Highlanders made a much better living in Canada than they could have had at home. Some were very successful indeed. John Alexander MacDonald, who became the first prime minister of the whole of Canada in 1867 (when the different provinces were brought together) was the son of a Sutherland crofter.

Many Highlanders were successful also in Australia. It was becoming popular with emigrants in the 1820s and it attracted more than Canada in the 1850s and 1860s. Highlanders liked working on Australian sheep runs. For example, Niel Black, the son of a farmer in Argyll, went out in 1839 to the colony of Victoria (a part of Australia which attracted many Scots). He bought a sheep run which he named Glenormiston. Almost all his workers and their wives were Highlanders. They knew how to look after animals, were used to loneliness and wide open spaces and found it easier to accept life on a sheep station than people from towns did. But they were not used to the endless plains, without a mountain to be seen, or the heat and the brilliant sunlight. A great problem of Australian sheep farmers was that their men often bolted (ran away) and even some of Niel Black's Highlanders did this. Some of the bolters made their way to Melbourne, which was becoming the Australian city with the greatest number of Scots. It had its own Highland games, as did many places in Canada, so that people could remember their old homes thousands of miles away in Sutherland or Uist or Glengarry. Songs they wrote also reminded them of home, such as the Canadian Boat Song:

> From the lone shieling of the misty island
> Mountains divide us, and the waste of seas—
> Yet still the blood is strong, the heart is Highland,
> As we in dreams behold the Hebrides.

8   The Highlands Today

If you visit the Highlands of Scotland perhaps it will be on a motoring tour or a camping holiday. Every summer thousands of tourists come to see the grandeur of the mighty Cuillin mountains in Skye or the softer colours of lower hillsides reflected in the sparkling blue lochs, or to watch from beaches of pure white sand as the sun sets in the west into the Atlantic Ocean. You may stop for the night at little whitewashed houses by the roadside carrying 'Bed and Breakfast' notices. There you will get the kind welcome for which Highlanders are famous. You will admire the modern furniture and fittings, which have been paid for by the visitors of previous years. You will enjoy the electric light and heat brought by the North of Scotland Hydro Electric Board even to clusters of houses miles from the nearest village. You are staying at a croft house, which may still have a little plot of land attached to it. But you will be very lucky if you find your host going out in the morning to work the croft. Most crofts are too small to be worth farming nowadays. The lochside or valley from which your host's great-grandfather had to move on to the croft may still have sheep grazing on it. Or, because the sheep were not profitable, it may have been sold to the Forestry Commission and be covered by trees. Not many men are needed to look after sheep or forests. So what does your host do during the winter when all the tourists have gone home? And where have his children got jobs?

Ever since the clearances Highlanders have accepted that many of them must leave home to find work. And for almost as

Opposite: *Oil production platform, 'Highland One', leaving Nigg to be towed to the Forties Oil Field, 1974*

long government has spent money to try to make work for as many of them as possible in the Highlands. Grants to build new boats have helped to make the north-west coast of Scotland a very important fishing centre, with large fleets sailing out of such ports as Mallaig, Lochinver and Kinlochbervie. The Highlands and Islands Development Board has lent money to allow Highlanders to start small businesses like hotels and tweed mills. Government money has encouraged firms to set up a few large factories in the Highlands, such as the paper pulp mill near Fort William and the aluminium smelter at Invergordon.

These efforts have never been enough to provide jobs for all the Highlanders, but some people think that North Sea Oil may at last do this. At each oil well a production platform is needed. This platform has to be several hundred feet high, as its top is above the surface and its base lies on the sea bed. Many lochs and firths around the North of Scotland are near the oil fields and have deep enough water for the floating out of these huge platforms. The first platform to be built in the Highlands, named 'Highland One', was completed in 1974 at Nigg on the Cromarty Firth and safely towed out to the Forties Oil Field. The questions which are now being asked are how many jobs will be created in the Highlands by North Sea Oil, how long will they last and how many of the jobs will be filled by Highlanders?

How Do We Know?

When he is finding out about events in the past the historian likes to be able to read accounts by people who were actually there at the time. He calls these 'primary sources'. The Napier Commission, who toured the Highlands in 1883, spoke to many crofters and printed what they said word for word in the 'Report of the Royal Commission into the Condition of Crofters and Cottars in the Highlands and Islands of Scotland' (1884). It is very interesting to hear how a crofter described the clearances many years ago. But this is only one side of the story: it is also interesting to read how the Highland landowners behaved, and the estate papers of two landowners have been published by the Scottish History Society. They are the 'Argyll Estate Instructions 1771–1805', edited by Eric R. Cregeen, and 'Papers on Sutherland Estate Management 1802–1816', edited by R.J. Adam. Also of importance to the historian when studying this period are the 'Statistical Account of Scotland' (usually called the 'Old Statistical Account'), which contains accounts of each Highland parish in the 1790s, written by the minister, and the 'New Statistical Account of Scotland', which contains parish accounts for the 1840s. You may be able to see these in your local library.

There are also many books written after the clearances. Some of these blame the landlords for the suffering of the Highlanders, such as 'The Highland Clearances' by John Prebble (Secker and Warburg, 1963). Others defend the landowners and describe the many problems they had. One such book is 'The Leviathan of Wealth' by Eric Richards (Routledge, 1973), which describes how the Sutherland family used their great wealth to try to find a living on the coast for the people who were cleared from the straths.

To understand the clearances we need to know about the problems which the Highlanders faced. Two books which explain these problems well are 'The Highland Economy 1750–1850' by Malcolm Gray (Oliver & Boyd, 1957) and 'After the Forty-Five' by A.J. Youngson (Edinburgh University Press, 1973).

'The Scots Overseas' by Gordon Donaldson (Hale, 1966) shows what happened to some of the Highlanders who emigrated.

Things To Do

1. Read again the extracts from the letters written by Captain Edward Burt describing life in the Highlands about 1730 in Chapter 1. Draw pictures to illustrate the scenes he describes.

2. Imagine you are a Highland minister in the 1790s, compiling a description of your parish for the 'Old Statistical Account'. Write part of the account which explains how hard it is for the people to make a living and what the sheep farm which has recently been started by a breeder from the Scottish Borders does to them.

3. Using a road atlas, draw a map of the main highland roads today. Show in a special colour the roads which were built by Thomas Telford in the early nineteenth century. You will find out which they were by looking at the map on page 34.

4. Stage the trial of Patrick Sellar in class. You will have to decide how many witnesses are to give evidence for and against him. One member of the class will have to act as the judge, one as the advocate (lawyer) accusing Sellar and another as the advocate defending him. All these people will have to think carefully about the evidence given in Chapter 4 and, if possible, in some of the books listed in 'How do we know?'

5. Imagine you are a newspaper reporter touring the Highlands towards the end of 1847, when the potato crop has failed for the second year running. Write a story for your paper describing the misery you have seen, what is being done to try to help the people and why many are having to leave home and make a new life far away.

6. Read again the account of the attempt to evict the crofters of Sollas, North Uist, in 1849. Make a picture or a frieze showing what happened.

7. Imagine you are a Highlander who has emigrated with his family to Canada in the 1850s. A Canadian newspaper has said that too many Highlanders are arriving. Write a letter to the paper

explaining why you had to leave the Highlands and describing how you are managing to make a living.

8. Imagine you are a crofter in the parish of Braes, Skye. You are addressing the Napier Commission in 1883. Explain why you want more land and why some of your friends were so angry a year ago that they took part in the attack on the police in the 'Battle of the Braes'.

9. Write a letter from a Highland landlord to a newspaper explaining why he must evict his tenants. Then write a reply from one of the evicted tenants.

10. Hold a class discussion on the case for the landlords and the case for the crofters.

Glossary

aggrieved, injured
agitator, man who stirs up trouble
apprehended, arrested
arable, suitable for ploughing to plant crops
arrears, behindhand
bannock, bun made of oats
bard, singer and story-teller
biased, in favour of one side rather than another
bludgeon, thick stick
Bonaparte, Napoleon Bonaparte, the French Emperor
bothy, hut
brae, hillside
burly, stout, sturdy
clan, a group of families under one chief
clansman, member of a clan
commission, committee to enquire into something
coronach, funeral chant
crabbed, rough, unnatured
creel, basket for carrying fish, kelp, etc.
croft, small farm
defile, narrow passage
destitution, being without any money or food
dirk, dagger
doleful, sad
dyke, stone wall (also ditch)
emigrant, person who leaves home to make a new life abroad
eviction, putting people out of their homes or off their land
ewe, female sheep
excess, amount too much
factor, man who manages an estate for the owner
feeder, man who fattens up sheep for market
flail, stick used for threshing corn

flitting, removal

greeting, crying

haugh, field, pasture

heath, moor used for pasture

identity, individuality (the shepherds could recognise each sheep)

intimate, make known

kail, vegetable like cabbage, used for making soup

kelp, seaweed, or the ash formed by burnt seaweed

kiln, oven

kind, goods

laird, Scottish landowner

lamentation, noise of sorrow

lease, agreement to rent

loch, lake

lot, piece of land

mania, madness

manse, the minister's house

Michaelmas, St Michael's Day, 29 September

moose, type of deer found in North America

motley, mixed, varied

packet service, regular service of ships

peat, decayed vegetable matter in the ground which is cut up, dried and used for fuel

petition, signed letter asking for something

portly, stout, bulky

press gang, gang which captured men to serve as sailors in the Royal Navy

privateer, privately owned ship given permission to capture the ships of enemy countries

privies, lavatories, toilets

proprietor, owner

providence, God's care

revenue cutter, ship used by customs men to search for smugglers

rig, long strip of earth in a field

scone, a flat bun

sheriff-substitute, judge in the sheriff court, which sits in every county to hear important cases

shieling, hut beside the high pastures used by cattle in summer

six-pointer, stag with six points on its antlers

skean dhu, dagger worn inside the top of man's stockings when he is wearing the kilt

smearing, rubbing tar and butter into the fleece of a sheep to protect it from maggots

strath, valley

summons, order to appear before a judge

temper of mind, mood

tenant, man renting a piece of land or a building from its owner

town, township, cluster of houses surrounded by fields

tract, area, expanse

trustee, someone who manages money matters for another person

warrant, legal document which gives permission for some action (such as arrest or eviction)

whey, part of the milk which remains when the rest forms curds, for example after cheese has been made

windward, side from which the wind is coming